Original title:
Tropical Daydreams

Copyright © 2025 Creative Arts Management OÜ
All rights reserved.

Author: Finn Donovan
ISBN HARDBACK: 978-1-80581-550-1
ISBN PAPERBACK: 978-1-80581-077-3
ISBN EBOOK: 978-1-80581-550-1

Serenade of the Coral Shore

With flip-flops squeaking, we dance on sand,
Giggles erupt as we build castles grand.
The ocean's tickles crash on our toes,
While seagulls squawk like they know our woes.

Sunburned noses and ice cream cones,
Witty remarks spun like tangled phones.
Crabs scuttle sideways with comical grace,
As we chase them laughing, a laugh-filled race.

Where Sunsets Paint the Sky

Colors collide in a fruity parade,
As we sip drinks, our worries allayed.
The sky bursts with laughter, a vibrant display,
Even the clouds seem to giggle and play.

A flamingo stumbles, all legs and no class,
While we snicker, our drinks now a glass.
A sunset so silly it makes our hearts soar,
Tomorrow awaits, can we take any more?

Echoes of Laughter on the Breeze

Waves whisper secrets, the palm trees sway,
Tickling the breezes, they join in the play.
A sandcastle pirate, with dreams made of foam,
Might just forget where he calls his home.

Children run wild, like puppies unleashed,\nSplashing in puddles, their giggles increased.
With every jump, they create such a mess,
Joy is contagious, it's pure happiness!

Harmony in a Horizon's Embrace

Bikini-clad wonders, we dance with delight,
Beach balls a-flying in the warm, golden light.
Unexpected tumbles provoke bursts of cheer,
As surfboards take flight, "Look out!" we all fear!

With flip and a flop, we glide on the waves,
Each sunset a canvas, our silliness saves.
Who knew a horizon could hold such a tease?
In laughter and joy, we find our sweet ease.

Silhouettes Against a Crimson Canvas

Palm trees sway as if they dance,
Coconuts roll, it's quite a chance.
A seagull squawks, what's his deal?
Wearing flip-flops, oh, what a feel!

Sunsets drip in hues so bold,
Champagne wishes, tales retold.
Crabs grabbing salsa with their claws,
Clumsy tourists, chuckles and applause.

A Symphony of Ocean Whispers

Waves hum tunes like a ukulele,
Beach balls bounce, just a bit crazy.
Sandcastles tumble with a puff,
Giggles float, this is enough!

Seashells whisper secrets sweet,
Flip flops dance to the wave's beat.
Dolphins leap with joyful hearts,
Making waves, they steal the arts.

Moonlight Glistens on Tropical Waters

Glowworms wink in the balmy night,
Mischievous crabs in their moonlight plight.
With pineapples swaying on the pier,
The drink's too strong, but never fear!

Stars overhead begin to play,
In a game of hide and seek, hooray!
A catamaran starts to sway,
And a parrot sings in disarray.

The Sweet Aroma of Paradise

Mangoes rolling off the trees,
Laughter floats upon the breeze.
A blender whirs with fruity cheer,
Accidentally adds some beer!

Tiki torches glowing bright,
Everyone's dancing through the night.
In this paradise of fun,
The party's just begun, oh hun!

Whispers of the Island Breeze

Parrots squawk with great delight,
While crabs do a silly dance by night.
The breeze is a tickle, oh what a tease,
As I chase my hat blown by the trees.

The waves laugh loud as they splash the shore,
A sunburned tourist shrieks, 'No more!'
Sandcastles wobble, then tumble down,
As seagulls laugh, stealing my crown.

Sunlit Shores and Silken Skies

Bikini-clad friends strike silly poses,
While sunbaked noses bloom like roses.
A beach ball flies, someone yells, 'Heads up!'
And juice spills over my fancy cup.

Sun hats laugh as they sail away,
Chasing flip-flops in a quirky play.
Laughter echoes under the sun's kiss,
Who knew paradise could be this bliss?

Lush Canopies and Liquid Light

Underneath the leaves, we throw a feast,
Mangoes fall, they're late for the east!
A monkey swings, with a cheeky grin,
And steals my snack—where do I begin?

The vines are tangled; it's quite absurd,
As I trip over, that is my word.
Rain comes splashing with giggles galore,
Making puddles, who could ask for more?

Dance of the Coconut Palms

Coconuts bounce like balls in the breeze,
While palm fronds sway with the greatest ease.
A tall guy slips on a smooth sea shell,
As laughter erupts—oh, what a spell!

In this lush paradise, jokes come alive,
Where grasshoppers dance and the crabs jive.
Life's a party that won't stop today,
Grab your shades, let's frolic and play!

A Retreat to Colorful Shores

Under a sun that wears a grin,
The waves invite us to jump in.
Sandy toes and laughter wide,
Shells are treasures where secrets hide.

Cocktails shake, umbrellas sway,
Seagulls squawk and steal our tray.
With a wink, the fish swim past,
In this bliss, troubles don't last.

Pulses of Nature's Symphonic Caress

The breeze plays tunes from big palm trees,
Nature's rhythm sways with ease.
Lemonade stands shout out their deals,
While sunburned skin squeals with squeals.

Crabs dance sideways on the sand,
And flip-flops lead us hand in hand.
A chorus of frogs join the mob,
As we chuckle while tossing the blob.

Kaleidoscope of Island Memories

A hammock sways, a gentle tease,
Where dreams are spun from coconut leaves.
Bananas split with creamy delight,
We giggle at the fireflies' flight.

The color wheel of sunset glows,
As a duck quacks at evening shows.
Footprints dance in the gooey sand,
We've become the island's merry band.

The Fragrance of Salt and Sweetness

The air's a cocktail of sea and cake,
As flavors whirl and laughter quake.
Pineapple hats wobble on heads,
While jellyfish do the cha-cha in beds.

Mangoes bounce like corks on waves,
With punchlines floating, the humor saves.
Cracking jokes under star-lit skies,
With twinkling stars that laugh and rise.

Rhapsody of a Seaside Reverie

Seagulls giggle, dancing high,
Crabs in tuxedos scuttle by,
A beach ball bounces, takes a flight,
Waves crack jokes in pure delight.

Sandy castles, moats of fun,
Shells like treasures, one by one,
Flip-flops squawk with every step,
Sunburned noses, what a pep!

Sunhats twirl in playful glee,
Ice cream drips, oh dear, oh me!
Laughter echoes, kids at play,
Sandy giggles rule the day.

With all the sun and sea, we find,
A beach where worries slip behind,
In this mirthful, bright parade,
Life's a jest, and we're the braid.

Footprints in the Warm Sand

Footprints etch stories on the shore,
Each step a giggle, hear them roar,
Waves tickle toes with a splashy kiss,
Sandcastles wobble in pure bliss.

Sunburned backs, a lobster hue,
Suntan lotion spills, oh whose?
Umbrellas whirl in a breezy spin,
Beach balls flying, where to begin?

Seashells hide secrets, whispers low,
Why does seaweed always grow?
Flipping flops on, then off again,
Who needs plans when fun's the gain?

Chasing crabs who scuttle free,
"Catch me if you can!" They plea,
Footprints fade, but laughter stays,
Memories made in sandy bays.

Whispers of the Coconut Breeze

Coconuts laughing in the trees,
Swinging gently with the breeze,
Palm fronds wave like playful hands,
Whispers tickle sun-kissed sands.

Lemons lounging in a drink,
Sipping sunshine, what to think?
Pineapples wearing shades so bright,
Join the party, it's a sight!

Bananas slip, oh, what a fall,
Mangoes gather for a ball,
Fruits in hats, such jolly cheer,
Life's a feast when friends are near.

Day ends with a wink and sway,
As stars peek out to join the play,
With giggles echoing through the trees,
Nighttime dances with the breeze.

Mirage of Sunlit Shores

Mirages shimmer, dreams unwind,
Sun-kissed moments, bliss defined,
Waves lull us with a sweet refrain,
Dancing shadows, playful gain.

Locals share old tales with flair,
Of fish that wear a sailor's wear,
Laughter lightens every load,
As sunbeams sketch a golden road.

Shells that croon a gentle tune,
Underneath the laughing moon,
Sandwiched sunbathers dream away,
As time just giggles in its play.

The last wave rolls, the sun will go,
But still, we bask in the glow,
With funny tales and cheerful throng,
In this paradise, we all belong.

Shimmering Horizons in Soft Hues

In a land where coconuts dance,
The palm trees sway in a silly trance.
Bikinis flip and flip-flops slide,
Everyone's laughing in the sunny tide.

Seagulls squawk with a cheeky grin,
Stealing snacks from your picnic bin.
A little child slips in the sand,
His sunburned nose just looks so grand.

Sippin' on drinks with tiny umbrellas,
Sharing gossip like giggling fellows.
The sun slips low, but who really cares?
We'll take our naps in lounge chair lairs.

As twilight paints the beach in gold,
We tell tall tales that never get old.
With laughter echoing through warm nights,
Life's just better with these silly sights.

The Call of the Island Spirits

Whispers float on the salty breeze,
While crabs do cha-cha with crabby ease.
A parrot yells, 'Try my new jam!'
The locals chuckle, 'He's such a ham!'

Waves crash gently, with a wobbly thunk,
A beach ball collides with someone's trunk.
The rhythm of laughter fills the air,
As a sunburned fellow strikes a pose with flair.

Dancing shadows beneath the moon,
A hula girl shakes, making us swoon.
But watch out! Here comes a flying fish,
With a splash, it joins our funny wish.

Mischievous spirits in every giggle,
Pranking tourists, causing them to wiggle.
In this paradise where silliness reigns,
We follow the laughter — it never wanes!

Over the Edge of the Aqua Dream

On the dock, we launch a grand plan,
To catch some waves like a true wild man.
But with one slip, in we go,
Flailing arms, oh what a show!

Colors burst under the hot sun's beam,
A jellyfish joins in our swimming team.
We shout and yell, 'Don't touch that thing!'
But thrill-seekers laugh and start to swing.

The splash contest has begun, you see,
With judges snickering, sipping their tea.
A belly flop sends waves high and wide,
While giggles spiral in the jumping tide.

As we float and drift on this waterway,
Dreams of sea monsters in funny play.
With each wave, new tales to weave,
We'll cherish the chaos, never to leave.

Prismatic Light on the Water's Edge

Sunrise paints the sky with a grin,
With beach towels strewn where fun begins.
A dog runs by with two flip-flops,
While surfers prepare with delicate hops.

Sandcastles guarded by vigilant kings,
While a kid faces off with a screeching swing.
The tide rolls in, and so does a wave,
Who knew 'beach day' could be this brave?

Flip over your drink, oh what a mess!
But cheers erupt, no room for distress.
As dolphins jump, putting on a show,
We all join in with shouts of 'Whoa!'

The sun dips low, painting all in gold,
We share our stories, funny and bold.
In this laughter-filled, radiant light,
We find joy, making memories bright.

Reverberations of Island Lullabies

A parrot squawks out of tune,
While crabs are doing a jittery dance.
The coconuts drop with a boom,
As the palm trees giggle in advance.

The waves wear shorts and flip-flops,
They surf with style, oh so bold.
The sun winks from its cloudy tops,
While the beach chairs tell tales of old.

The seaweed sways like a diva,
Inviting fish to join the bash.
In this party, the starfish strive,
To outshine the dolphin's flashy splash.

With sandcastles reaching for the bright,
And seagulls stealing snacks with glee.
The island rocks, from day till night,
In a comical jubilee.

Beneath the Canopy of Daylight

Under the trees, the monkeys swing,
Trading jokes with the buzzing bees.
A turtle tries to do the cha-cha,
But trips on roots, oh what a tease!

The sunbeams play hide and seek,
As lizards flash their fancy coats.
A goofball frog starts to speak,
Ribbiting promises of boats.

The air is thick with laughter's scent,
While butterflies don hats of flair.
With every giggle and comment,
The jungle dances without a care.

Beneath this roof, the whimsy grows,
A harmony of giggles and cheer.
For in this wild place, anything goes,
Where silly dreams drift ever near.

Sunset Collage of Sky and Sea

The sun drips like a melting cone,
Painting the sky in fruity hues.
As clouds play tic-tac-toe alone,
While turtles recite silly news.

Flamingos strike a pose for fun,
Making shadows dance on the sand.
The horizon blushes, all undone,
As the waves clap with a light hand.

Children chase the sunshine fade,
In a game of tag with the breeze.
While fish in schools of colors parade,
Trying to tickle the ocean's knees.

With laughter echoing through the air,
And shells that laugh when you pick them up.
The sunset's giggles have a flair,
Drizzled in joy from the golden cup.

Glistening Hopes on the Horizon

As day ends, stars begin to play,
Twinkling mischievously like kids.
The moon wears sunglasses at bay,
Sipping coconut drinks with lids.

The night whispers funny little tales,
To seashells listening with intent.
As tides rise up in slapstick trails,
Making the shore a playground, content.

The hammock swings with gentle grace,
While fireflies buzz with soft delight.
In this dreamy, magical space,
The moonbeams dance till the morning light.

With every twinkle and silly sigh,
Hope glistens bright like sea foam's kiss.
On this horizon, oh my oh my,
Adventure never ends in bliss.

Daydreams Born from Waves

A mermaid in flip-flops prances by,
Her laugh makes the seagulls dance and fly.
Coconuts in hand, she stirs the sea,
Sand castles rise, a kingdom wild and free.

Breezes carry whispers from afar,
A dolphin slicked up with sunlit bra.
Sand crabs in tuxedos march in line,
While palm trees sway, sipping on sunshine.

Sunburned turtles all gather by,
For a beach party under the sky.
They juggle beach balls with such delight,
While the sun waves goodbye, saying goodnight.

Laughter echoes over the gentle sound,
Waves crash like laughter, bouncing around.
Daydreams sprout, each one a little strange,
In this paradise, we'll never change.

Dreamlike Palette of Island Colors

The sun drips orange, almost like cheese,
As parakeets squawk in grand little tease.
A painter on the shore mixes the blue,
With hibiscus petals, a most vibrant hue.

Bananas wear hats, it's quite the sight,
While fish in tiny tuxedos swim right.
The ocean winks, a playful old friend,
Mixing the colors as they blend and bend.

Limes roll like marbles on the sand,
While pineapples tango, perfectly planned.
If laughter's the diet, we're all so full,
This artist's palette, a whimsical pull.

Dreamlike strolls amid vibrant blooms,
Where every step sways, and heart resumes.
In this wacky world, no one's grown-up,
Just living the color from coconut cups.

Luminous Echoes of Tides Beyond

The waves hum softly a giggly tune,
As glowing jellyfish float, they balloon.
Starfish plot mischief, with smiles so wide,
While seaweed giggles, in laughter they hide.

Crabs set the stage for a dance-off spree,
With flip-flops on claws, they dance with glee.
Splashing around, blue bubbles they chase,
In this watery wonderland, it's a race.

The moon spills laughter across ocean blue,
Reflecting dreams as if they were new.
Each wave that crashes tells tales of fun,
Beneath the bright glow of the shimmery sun.

Echoes of laughter seep through the tides,
As clams sing solos where sand royalty slides.
In this bubble of joy, worries are few,
As we dance with the waves, all fresh and new.

The Sweetness of Plantain Skies

Up in the sky, ripe plantains float,
Giggles of monkeys on a banana boat.
They swing 'round trees, wearing silly frowns,
Laughing and tossing their playful crowns.

Balloons shaped like fruit drift on by,
Blue skies painted with tunes of a pie.
The sun beams down, all laughter and cheer,
As islanders toss water, their joy sincere.

With every splash, whimsical stories arise,
Fish dressed in pajamas take to the skies.
Seashells all chatter about the affair,
As kites painted like fruit dance in the air.

At day's sweet end, the stars start to peek,
Whispers of fun fill the night with a sneak.
In a world where silliness rules and flies,
We relish the wonders of plantain skies.

Secrets Held by Exotic Blooms

In the garden, secrets grin,
Petals giggle, where to begin?
A parrot steals the show with flair,
While the sunflowers just stare.

Bumblebees with clumsy dance,
Fumble through a flower's chance,
They laugh and buzz, a busy crew,
In a world where gossip grew.

A tulip whispers to a rose,
"Did you hear about that nose?"
The daisies roll in fits of glee,
As the lilies guard the tea.

Lettuce leaves begin to tease,
With tales of wind and rustling trees,
Each bloom's giggle floats on high,
In this garden, laughter's spry.

Driftwood Dreams and Distant Shores

Driftwood tales on sandy strands,
Mermaids play in glittered bands,
Seagulls squawk, they have their chats,
And crabs perform in tiny hats.

A coconut rolls, oh what a sight,
It dreams of sailing day and night,
With barnacles as its friends,
It knows the beach, that's where it ends.

Waves send messages, quite absurd,
"Did you hear the latest word?"
Turtles nod in solemn tune,
As shells all sing beneath the moon.

Shells too shy to join the jest,
Hide away, they know the rest,
But in the tides, the humor frolics,
While seaweed laughs at ocean's chronicles.

Canvas of the Ocean's Palette

A painter's brush in ocean's sway,
Colors splash, in playful play,
Waves giggle with hues of blue,
As fish turn cartwheels just for you.

Coral reefs are fancy hats,
Dancing with the fishy chaps,
Plankton holds a late-night show,
While jellyfish steal the glow.

Stars above wink down with glee,
Their twinkling makes waves fancy-free,
Octopuses juggle in a spree,
With eight-armed grace, oh what a sight to see.

But when the tide decides to leave,
All colors fade, but then we believe,
That under currents, art will bloom,
Creating laughter in each room.

Caressed by the Warmth of Dusk

As dusk arrives, the sun's last wink,
It nudges stars to come, to drink,
Crickets chirp, their songs a jest,
While fireflies glow in silken vest.

The palm trees sway with graceful sighs,
Whispering secrets to the skies,
Chasing shadows in the breeze,
While someone trips over the keys.

The horizon blushes, just for fun,
As laughter bubbles, one by one,
A beach ball rolls and steals the show,
And sandcastles begin to grow.

Night blankets dreams with cozy wraps,
But not before a series of mishaps,
In this warm haze, joy does bask,
While the moon's grin is all we ask.

Coral Reefs and Golden Sands

A crab in shades, dancing on the shore,
While fish gossip about the ocean's lore.
Seashells giggle, caught in the tide,
As seagulls laugh on their merry ride.

Starfish debate who wears the best glow,
Sandcastles look smug, with claims they know.
The tide sneaks up, giving all a splash,
And everyone laughs at the water's rash.

An octopus winks, ink clouds in the deep,
He dreams of a party where sea creatures leap.
Clams sing barbershop with a touch of sass,
While dolphins perform a synchronized dance.

Bikini-clad mermaids join in the fun,
Slipping on seaweed, in the sun they run.
Under the waves, a riotous scene,
Where laughter bubbles, and all's serene!

Azure Waves of Morning Bliss

A coconut falls, with a comic thud,
Taking out a crab, now covered in mud.
The sun peeks in with a wink and a grin,
Saying, 'Let the beach games truly begin!'

Surfboards tumble in a sandy embrace,
As kids giggle while they try to race.
A rogue wave sneaks, causing quite a flop,
Sending beach balls high, then making them drop.

Umbrellas spin like a wild carousel,
As picnic ants tell their own tales to tell.
Ice cream melts faster, drizzling down toes,
While sunhats fly off like kites in the blows.

Laughter erupts as the beach towels flip,
A sandcastle prince takes a lazy dip.
In the azure waves, joy is the tune,
Under the chuckling, bright afternoon.

Melodies of Mango Orchards

Mangoes drop like notes from trees so tall,
Landing on heads, what a fruity brawl!
Birds whistle tunes that make ripened fruit sway,
As squirrels join in the nutty ballet.

A parrot rehearses its stand-up routine,
With punchlines so ripe, you know what I mean!
The breeze carries whispers of laughter and cheer,
While sun rays tickle, drawing everyone near.

Orchard picnics turn into jam sessions,
With juicy debates over fruit's best impressions.
A hammock swings low, enticing a nap,
But is rudely interrupted by a bee with a map.

Fruits in a frenzy, the day's laughter swells,
With each bite of mango, the orchard repels.
In this fruity dream where the laughter won't stop,
It's a melody sweet, an orchard-tastic hop!

Beneath the Swaying Palm Fronds

Palm trees gossip about the sun's big hat,
While coconuts share tales of where they're at.
Fronds swaying gently, like they're doing a jig,
As lizards pose like they're hoping for a gig.

Sandy toes shimmy with a rhythm so bright,
While flip-flops battle, squeaking in delight.
A crab in a top hat crochets with flair,
Making beach fashion a spectacle rare.

Sunbathers chuckle as sunscreen spills wide,
Giving glistening skin a comedic glide.
Snorkels bobbing to a silly refrain,
As beach chairs join in with a creak and a gain.

Under the palms, the laughter flows fast,
Turning the heat into moments that last.
A paradise found where the fun never ends,
With memories made beneath swaying fronds and friends.

Serenity of the Surfing Sands

Waves crash down like giggling friends,
Seagulls dance, their laughter lends.
A crab does the cha-cha, quite absurd,
As beach balls bounce, the fun is stirred.

Umbrella hats are all the rage,
Sandy noses on this fun-filled stage.
Sunblock fails, a slippery feat,
We laugh as flip-flops dance on our feet.

Shells tell secrets in salty whispers,
Sunburned shoulders act like twisters.
Cool drinks spill in a sandy leak,
Life's a joke, we laugh and peek.

Oh, how the coconut jokes do roll,
A parrot's squawk, a comic goal!
With laughter echoing, we'll never tire,
On this beach, joy's a constant fire.

Blushing Sunset over Paradise

The sun blushes like a bashful child,
Transforming the sky, wild and mild.
Cocktails clink like cheers of glee,
While beach bums grin, just you and me.

Palm trees sway with a cheeky sway,
Whispering secrets of the day.
As shadows stretch and silly pose,
The horizon bursts like a giggle's prose.

Fluffy clouds compete for a crown,
While flip-flops flail and some fall down.
With sherbet skies and fruity treats,
Life feels like dance, oh, isn't it sweet?

As the sun dips down, a clownfish leaps,
Into moments the laughter keeps.
With silly grins, we wave goodnight,
To the blushing sky, pure delight.

Dreams Carried by the Trade Winds

Whimsical breezes play hide and seek,
Tickling your toes, oh, how they sneak!
A kite soars up with a prankster's flair,
As we tumble and roll without a care.

Mangoes spill like rain from the trees,
Sticky sweet, carried on the breeze.
A monkey swings with a cheeky grin,
As if he knows the fun's about to begin.

The waves send whispers of laughter near,
In this paradise, there's nothing to fear.
With each gust, a chuckle's born,
As joy and mischief dance at dawn.

Clouds drift by, wearing hats of fun,
Painting dreams 'til the day is done.
With giggles lodged in the sandy shore,
In this playful land, there's always more.

Footprints in a Surreal Oasis

In a land where the poppies giggle bright,
Footprints wander left and right.
A frog wearing shades leaps to the beat,
While sunflowers twirl, oh, so sweet.

Watermelon slices float like boats,
Cactus jokes, the desert gloats.
Camel drivers challenge the wind,
With laughter that makes the dull unpinned.

Mirages play tricks, our eyes can't fight,
As shadows twist in the golden light.
Flip-flops squawk on ground so odd,
While funny hats make the sun applaud.

In this surreal place, let's spin a tale,
Of wild winds that dance like a whale.
With each step we leave a laugh behind,
As footprints of joy are always kind.

A Journey Through the Velvet Heat

In a hammock swinging high,
Twirling thoughts of coconut pie,
My thoughts drift on a lizard's tail,
As sweat beads dance like a tiny snail.

Beneath a sun that blinks and winks,
The parrot sings while the monkey drinks,
I trip on dreams of bright pink rays,
And giggle at the sun's odd ways.

The breeze is hot but cheeky cool,
Dancing with the tropical school,
A cloud flips off the golden light,
And then it rains confetti bright.

With every sip of mango juice,
I laugh at life, let visions loose,
For in this heat, I find my charm,
Underneath the sun's warm arm.

Emerald Canopies and Starry Nights

Up in the trees, the coconuts sway,
With dreams of pirates that never stay,
A starlit sky, a leafy screen,
The moon's a glow-in-the-dark marine.

Sipping drinks that taste like delight,
I wonder if sloths ever take flight,
The owls grin wide, with secret glee,
As I dance with the breeze so free.

The fireflies flash their tiny lights,
While I give my sandals tiny bites,
Laughter echoes through the leafy maze,
While I contemplate my wobbly phase.

From twinkling stars to rustling trees,
I twirl with laughter, shake off the bees,
In this canopy of joy, I find,
That silly dreams are oh so kind!

Waves of Passion on Sandy Shores

On sandy shores, where crabs compete,
I trip over shells, it's quite a feat,
The seagulls squawk in jest and play,
While I slip on sunscreen—hip hooray!

The waves crash like a joke gone wrong,
With frothy laughter, they sing their song,
I try to surf but meet my doom,
As water greets me with a boom.

Flip-flops fly like a jet on the run,
As sand gets stuck—oh, what fun!
A hoot and howl by the beach bonfire,
While marshmallows melt in a goopy choir.

With salty kisses from the breeze,
I frolic like a child with ease,
And in their dance, my wishes soar,
On a shore where giggles forever pour.

The Spirit of the Sea and Sky

Waves sway and shimmer, what a sight,
Like jellybeans dancing in the night,
The sea whispers jokes, silly and bright,
As clouds float by, feeling just right.

With fish that jump like they've won the game,
I chuckle aloud as I shout their name,
A crab waves back, it's quite a show,
While gulls play tag—they're too fast, you know.

Under the sky that chuckles and rolls,
I chase down dreams that tickle my soles,
The ocean hums a playful tune,
As I pretend I'm a big balloon.

From sea to sky, joy unconfined,
In this playful world, I unwind,
Where laughter floats on each gentle sigh,
And every moment gleams like the sky.

Dance of the Hibiscus Petals

Petals twirl on the gentle breeze,
As if they're dancing with such ease.
A bee buzzes by in a silly way,
A party of colors, come join the fray!

Laughter echoes through the quiet field,
While flowers in bloom, their secrets revealed.
Can't tell if it's a garden or a show,
With petals and giggles stealing the glow!

Beneath the Banyan's Shade

Underneath branches that twist and twine,
A squirrel fashions acorns into a shrine.
A picnic unfolds, sandwiches galore,
With ants joining in, who could ask for more?

Chasing the shadows of daylight's delight,
As laughter erupts, oh what a sight!
A cheeky lizard, with quick little feet,
Dares all to dance to the rhythm of heat!

Secrets of the Turquoise Waters

Hidden beneath waves of shimmering hues,
Fish spin and twirl, donning their best shoes.
A crab with a wink shares a laugh with the tide,
While seashells gossip, oh what a ride!

The dolphins chuckle — it's a splashy affair,
Juggling seaweed without a care.
A mermaid appears with a grin so wide,
Offering treasures from the ocean's pride!

Radiant Frangipani Nights

The stars wink down like playful sprites,
While frangipanis spark under moonlit nights.
A frog begins croaking a melody grand,
Conducting the symphony in the sand!

With fireflies twirling, it's a luminous show,
As the breeze carries whispers from below.
Crickets chime in, they're quite the band,
With petals as cushions, we groove in the sand!

Serenity Wrapped in a Salty Embrace

A sunburned crab did a tap dance,
While locals giggled at its prance.
A hammock swayed with each small breeze,
And laughter floated through the trees.

An ice cream cone fell on a cat,
It licked it up, then sat down flat.
The seagulls squawked a silly tune,
As sun hats danced beneath the moon.

A fish in shorts took a stroll with flair,
While beach balls bounced without a care.
A mermaid tried to catch a wave,
But ended up just being brave.

In this paradise, where smiles ignite,
Every mishap shines a little light.
So grab a drink, let worries go,
And join the fun in this sunny show.

Chimeras of Warm Island Nights

The moonlit shore called for a chase,
As geckos strutted in silly grace.
A lantern hung, just slightly crooked,
While little kids played, spirits hooked.

A dancing parrot dropped a beat,
It grooved with dolphins, oh so sweet.
Flip-flops flew when laughter blared,
As kooky games had all unprepared.

A coconut fell, a boom rang loud,
It startled the sunbathers' proud crowd.
They giggled and rolled in the sand,
As starfish cheered, a happy band.

Night's whimsical tales never tire,
With fireflies lit like playful choir.
So let the waves hold your delight,
In this realm of mirth, we take flight.

Mists of Blissful Escapes

Beneath the palms, a parrot pranks,
He mimics laughs, gives funny thanks.
A wave appeared, but missed its mark,
And left behind a jelly shark.

In floaty gear, the friends all glide,
While one misplaced his nose and cried.
A splash reveals a truth quite clear,
The water's warm, but jokes are dear.

A snorkeler laughed at a fishy stare,
As fins tickled, she felt a scare.
They swirled and twirled in a comic swirl,
In this ocean of giggles, they gave a twirl.

Each moment drips in salty cheer,
Where fun and folly disappear.
Escape with us, embrace the jest,
In this dreamy land, we find our rest.

Celestial Reflections in the Coral Sea

Stars peeked down at the frothy spree,
While crabs donned caps for the jubilee.
A splash from a seal brought roars of glee,
As moonlit waves danced so free.

The jellyfish glowed in colors bright,
Zigzagging through the shimmering light.
A silly shark tried to steal the show,
But fish laughed loud, 'Please take it slow!'

A beach ball bounced high in the air,
Landing on heads without a care.
Sandcastles churned in a giggling fight,
As waves came crashing into the night.

With every laugh, the world sways in cheer,
And trouble and frowns just disappear.
So swim with joy, and let spirits soar,
In this cosmic sea, we'll laugh evermore.

Chasing Shadows of Palm Trees

Beneath the palms, I chase the shade,
My flip-flops squeak, a grand parade.
The sunbeam zooms, so hot, so bright,
I trip on smiles, oh what a sight!

The shadows dance, they play and tease,
I laugh aloud, caught in the breeze.
A coconut falls, it lands on my head,
"Is this a fruit or a warm, soft bed?"

I wave to birds, they mock me so,
Their plumage bright, a rainbow show.
But as I slip, I feel no shame,
For in this game, we're all the same!

As laughter rings, the day grows long,
In this wild chase, I sing my song.
With every shadow, a story spun,
Under the palms, oh what a fun!

Thoughts Adrift on a Gentle Wave

The waves roll in, a playful breeze,
I float along, with such great ease.
A rubber duck sails, my trusty mate,
Together we plan a grand estate!

The sun shines down, so bright and bold,
My sunburned nose is a sight to behold.
I sip from coconuts, feeling quite spry,
While seagulls form a karaoke sky!

My thoughts drift off, just like a kite,
But wait! What's this? A jellyfish sight!
I jump and squawk, a comical dance,
With my rubber duck, we take a chance!

As laughter echoes across the shore,
I lose my hat and it starts to soar.
Yet on this wave, I find my groove,
In silly floats, I always move!

Hiding in the Floral Embrace

Amidst the blooms, I find my spot,
A daisy crown, a silly lot.
Bees buzz by, they chuckle too,
"You're quite the sight, who dressed you?"

The flowers sway, they tip and twirl,
In this garden, I spin and whirl.
With each petal's laugh, I feel so free,
A floral party just for me!

I hide away from boring chats,
Pretending to be a cat with hats.
But watch out now, I start to sneeze,
Those lovely blooms make me say "cheese!"

With smiles draped in colors bright,
I dance in petals, pure delight.
In floral realms, I'm never shy,
Just a jester with wings to fly!

A Rainbow of Sea and Sky

The sky paints hues of blue and gold,
While waves rush in with stories untold.
I ride the surf, a laugh so loud,
A jellyfish steals the local crowd!

As rainbows bloom on the ocean wide,
I wear my shades, I'm filled with pride.
Each splash of color, a wink to me,
"Look at my masterpiece, can you see?"

My friends all gather for shells and fun,
We build high castles, oh what a run!
But soon they fall, a sorry plight,
I guess the tide is a comical fright!

Yet in this splash of life so bright,
I find my joy, my heart takes flight.
With laughter soaring, the day feels spry,
In this rainbow world, we never say bye!

Fantasia of the Ocean's Breath

Salty air tickles my nose,
A seagull squawks, 'Hey, look at those!'
Flip-flops slapping, laughter flows,
As beach balls soar, the fun just grows.

Dancing crabs in a funky line,
They can move, it's a sight divine!
Waves crash in a splashy mime,
Who knew beach life could be so fine?

Sunburned noses all around,
Some wear funny hats that astound.
With each drink, silliness is found,
In this waveside circus, joy abounds.

Mermaids giggle, flip their tails,
As jellyfish become the sails.
Life's a beach; tell all the tales,
With laughter echoing through the gales.

Tranquil Gaze at Distant Clouds

Sipping coconuts beneath a tree,
Clouds parade like a comedy spree.
One looks like a duck, can't you see?
What a silly place this can be!

Banana leaves wave their green hands,
While ants march to their tiny bands.
A toucan sings, drawing big plans,
To snag a snack from the nearest stands.

Time drifts like a sleepy kite,
While worms dance, feeling just right.
A lizard breaks into a slight,
Dance-off—what a curious sight!

Giggles rise with the softest breeze,
As flowers blush with such great ease.
Nature's fun lays us at peace,
In this gaze, all worries cease.

Tales from the Water's Edge

Fish wear hats in the shimmering stream,
As frogs croak out a silly theme.
A snail with swagger, oh what a dream,
Here at the water's edge, life's a meme!

Turtles race in a slow-motion heat,
While dragonflies think they're quite neat.
Splashing kids can't find their feet,
In this watery playground, laughter's sweet.

Giggling otters glide and twist,
In a game of tag, they can't resist.
With each splash, the day's pure bliss,
Adventures found with every twist!

A crab scuttles, pinching heads,
While seaweed wraps around our threads.
Life's quirks dance as the sun spreads,
At the water's edge, fun never dreads.

Swaying to Nature's Soft Chorus

Palm trees sway in a rhythmic beat,
While a squirrel tries to find a seat.
Dancing beetles drag their feet,
In this natural show, life's a treat!

Wind whispers jokes like a best friend,
As flowers in laughter twist and bend.
A parrot squawks its message to send,
In nature's chorus, fun doesn't end.

Clouds bring laughter, a ticklish tease,
As raindrops fall like silly peas.
Giggling leaves dance in the breeze,
In this choir, we find such ease.

Life unravels in soft hums and sighs,
Where silly things come as a surprise.
Nature giggles, under bright skies,
A whimsical world, love amplifies.

Sunkissed Serenade of the Stars

The sun's a lazy lemon, bright,
It tickles toes, oh what a sight!
Palm trees sway, a quirky dance,
While crabs in bow ties take a chance.

Coconut hats atop our heads,
Laughter echoes, drops from beds.
Seagulls gossip, stealing fries,
As beach balls bounce towards the skies.

Shady spots, a hammock swing,
We sing off-key, we laugh and sling.
The waves, they clap, a friendly cheer,
To sound of waves and frozen beer.

When night descends, the stars poke fun,
They wink at us, oh what a run!
With moonlit dreams that swirl and glide,
We'll dance till dawn, our hearts our guide.

Voyage Through a Coconut Grove

In a boat made of fruit, we row,
Dodging crabs that put on a show.
Bamboo sticks and laughter mix,
While silly fish tease with their tricks.

Coconuts fall like clumsy balloons,
Each splat a laugh, a couple of tunes.
The parrots chat, all in a twist,
Who knew this grove would be such a list?

Banana waves make our heads spin,
We all wear shades; oh where to begin?
With sunburns that look like a map,
We giggle and flop in a feathery nap.

As time flies by on this fruity ride,
We'll toast to the fun with our arms open wide.
For every wave that splashes around,
Is another chuckle to be found!

The Colorful Canvas of Paradise

Painted skies with strokes so bold,
A canvas of giggles waiting to unfold.
Colors drip like melting ice,
In this land where nonsense is quite nice.

Fishes wearing funky hats,
Bananas laughing, giving high-fives to mats.
The ocean mouths jokes, it's such a hoot,
While crabs in shades strut in a suit.

Every sunset takes a bow,
Whispers the secrets of moth and cow.
With sparkly drinks in rainbow hues,
We sail on dreams and groovy blues.

Laughter echoes, the best kind of art,
In this wonderland, we play our part.
With paintbrushes made of sunshine rays,
We'll dance till the moon joins our plays.

Reflections on a Sea of Dreams

Mirror of water, oh what a sight,
Where the fish wear pajamas, what a delight!
Reflections giggle with dazzling glee,
As we sip on coconuts, just me and thee.

Waves roll in, with silly grins,
Making waves like quirky spins.
The sun on our toes makes us rise,
And clouds compete in the game of skies.

Here laughter floats like fluffy boats,
While even the turtles take silly votes.
In this kingdom of smiles, we rule the hour,
With tickles and snickers as our power.

As dusk arrives and dreams run wild,
We'll chase the stars, like a gleeful child.
With sleepy whispers, and giggles that beam,
Together we'll sail on a sea of dreams.

Sunrise over Coral Reefs

The sun peeks up, a giant yolk,
Fish swim by, whispering a joke.
Sea turtles dive with a splashy flair,
While crabs dance like they just don't care.

The dolphins giggle, making a scene,
A seagull swoops down, wearing a green.
As surfboards wobble on the sandy shore,
A coconut falls, and the laughter does pour.

Flip-flops squeak on the warm, wet sand,
Grinning like kids with a popsicle in hand.
Sunshine drips like honey from the skies,
Waves tickle toes, oh, what a surprise!

The day rolls out like an old beach towel,
With jellyfish joining in for a howl.
From coral to palm, the day's a delight,
In this splashy world, everything feels right.

Warm Embrace of Salted Air

A burger flips with a sizzle and pop,
Seagulls swoon, thinking they're top.
The breeze carries scents of fries and fun,
While sunbathers lounge, wishing for sun.

Kids build castles that are more like sand blobs,
While laughter erupts with each goofy sob.
Lobsters blush in the heat's warm embrace,
As sunscreen battles with a clumsy face.

Umbrellas flop like hats in the wind,
Beach games begin; who will win?
With each chuckle, the morning grows bright,
In this party of sun, everything's all right.

A crab steals a chip, oh what a sight,
Chasing laughter, till it's out of sight.
With salty kisses from the ocean's spray,
We dance and dive, oh what a day!

Nectar of the Setting Sun

As the sun dips low, it spills its gold,
Cocktails swirl with stories untold.
The horizon glows like a giant piña colada,
While palm trees sway, simply like nada.

Laughter floats like the smell of curry,
Sandcastles cringe as the tide starts to hurry.
Each sunset a canvas, painted so bright,
As fireflies burst forth like stars in the night.

Tiki torches flicker, casting a grin,
A mosquito mist visits folks by the din.
As the stars pop out, a chorus begins,
With ukuleles strumming sweetly like wins.

The day wraps up in a vibrant embrace,
With high-fives all around, it's a memorable place.
As new tales are spun under starry delight,
Who said sunsets were only for the night?

Melodies of the Island Breeze

Guitars tinkle like a playful cat,
Dancers twirl, oh, imagine that!
The breeze teases hair with a gentle touch,
While shimmery fish give a little hush.

A parrot squawks with a taste for style,
Wearing bright colors, oh, what a profile!
Children giggle as they chase their dreams,
In a whirl of rhythm, laughter streams.

Shells rattle like castanets in the sun,
As beachcombers hop, eager for fun.
A wink from a sand crab, a funny parade,
In this ocean party, memories are made.

With swaying palms, we sway to the beat,
In every whisper, the day feels sweet.
From sunrise to dusk, let humor unwind,
In this symphony, happiness we find.

Lush Horizons in My Mind

In a land where parrots laugh,
Sipping coconuts, having a blast.
The sun does a tango, bright and bold,
While lazy iguanas enjoy the gold.

Flip-flops dance in the balmy breeze,
Where jellyfish wear hats, if you please.
The sky spills colors, a fruity blend,
As my ice cream cone swirls, a bit unkempt.

Sweaty palms wave to banana trees,
Bees buzzing tunes like funky DJs.
Palm fronds gossip under the sun's glow,
While dancing flamingos steal the show.

And in this land of giggles and glee,
Even the crabs clap, proud as can be.
With waves that chuckle and tickle my feet,
My heart takes a dive, there's no retreat.

The Mango Moonlit Reverie

At night when the mangoes start to sway,
The moon's like a fruit, bright and gay.
Lemons giggle in silver beams,
While bananas plot mischievous schemes.

Kites made of laughter float on by,
Kiwis chuckle up in the sky.
Dreams drape over like soft, warm sand,
As jellybeans jive hand in hand.

Lemons splash in a bubble bath,
Taking turns on a coconut path.
While watermelon wedges wear little hats,
Under the gaze of the night sky chats.

Dancing shadows invite a smile,
The stars twinkle, let's stay a while.
With every sip of this sweet delight,
Mangoes whisper secrets through the night.

Serene Sands and Coconut Trees

On serene shores where coconuts chill,
Sandy castles take form with a thrill.
Children giggle, catching the tide,
While seagulls dive with a belly slide.

Sunbathers lay like hotdogs on plates,
Fruits roll like turtles, in funny states.
Fluffy clouds wear pajama pants,
As flip-flops tango in summer's dance.

Old crabs in shades play a game of chess,
While surfboards wish they could wear a dress.
Giggles echo, a bright serenade,
Hiding from shadows that softly invade.

And as the stars pop out one by one,
The party continues, oh what fun!
Coconut drinks spill laughter and cheer,
In this sandy paradise, life's crystal clear.

Driftwood Secrets by the Ocean

Driftwood sits with stories to share,
Whispering secrets of sea and air.
Shells giggle softly, keeping the peace,
As crabs trade jokes for a bit of fleece.

The ocean waves tap dance on the shore,
Seashells giggle, always wanting more.
Sun hats toss in a whimsical breeze,
While fish sneak peeks from behind the trees.

Watch the driftwood pull silly faces,
As sea cows parade in funny paces.
Tides swirl like dancers in a show,
While dolphins giggle, putting on a glow.

Then bogey down 'til dusk's gentle hand,
As the ocean waves wave their bands.
Under the starlit vastness up high,
Dreamy driftwood winks, oh so sly.

Colors of the Island Dawn

A parrot's squawk brightens the morn,
While a crab in shades of red is born.
Coconuts fall with a thud and a thump,
As locals rejoice with a whimsical jump.

Sunshine spills like a mango drink,
Making everyone pause and think.
With laughter that floats on a breeze so sweet,
Even the turtles tap their feet.

Vibrant blooms in a silly parade,
Each petal sporting a giant charade.
Hula skirts twirling under palm trees,
As the wind joins in, teasing with ease.

And in the sky, a kitefish flies,
Swimming through clouds with curious eyes.
Chasing the sun in a playful race,
Painting smiles on each sunny face.

Echoes of a Sun-Kissed Afternoon

Beneath the sun, the beach is alive,
Where sunscreen smells and seagulls dive.
Sandcastles rise, then crumble away,
As children giggle and splatter in play.

The waves whisper secrets of seashells rare,
With a surfboard floating without a care.
Each splash brings a chorus of shrill delight,
While surfboards dance in the golden light.

Ice cream melts faster than you can lick,
But oh, what a joy, it's a sweet little trick!
With flavors like banana and cotton candy,
The brain freeze hits, but it's totally dandy.

And if a dolphin stops by to say,
"Hey, come play!" in a splashy ballet,
You'll find that laughter's the language of fun,
In this sun-kissed world, where worries are none.

Palms Dancing to the Rhythm of Waves

Under the palms, the party ignites,
As coconuts sway with delight in the nights.
The breeze plays the bongos, a delightful tune,
While stars twinkle brightly, a natural boon.

Fishes in hats swim by with flair,
Even the lobsters decide to wear a pair!
The crabs join the conga, what a wild sight,
As waves keep the tempo, guiding the night.

Flip-flops are flying, shoes left behind,
With every misstep, folks laugh and unwind.
The rhythm of laughter cascades like the tide,
In a dance where all are invited to glide.

And balloons from a party float high in the sky,
To join in the fun, as they cheerfully fly.
So grab your friends, let's dance on the shore,
In this island disco, who could ask for more?

Enchanted Tides of a Summer Dream

The ocean swirls with giggles and glee,
As sea cucumbers plot their jubilee.
Jellyfish bloom like fireworks bright,
They sway to the music of waves in the night.

With a wink and a flip, a whale blows a kiss,
Creating a splash that's hard to miss.
Mermaids with tea parties, how very quaint,
While clams tell tales of wonder and paint.

Laughter ricochets as the sun dips low,
Magical shades like a shimmering show.
The stars join the dance, lighting up the night,
As coconuts nod in their carefree flight.

So let your worries drift away like a breeze,
In this enchanted world, where all hearts are at ease.
With every wave that crashes nearby,
A reason to smile, a reason to fly.

Fables of the Coconut Shell

Once a nut in the sun's warm glow,
Spoke of dreams and a brave, cool flow.
With a hat made of leaves, oh so neat,
He danced on the sand with bare feet.

With a laugh like a wave, he told a tale,
Of a pirate who lost his way by a snail.
'A treasure,' he said, 'just follow the breeze!'
While sipping on juice from his piece of cheese.

His parrot friend laughed, so loud and bright,
Claiming coconuts give the best flight.
With a flip and a flop, they launched from a mound,
But landed in sand, all giggles abound.

So next time a coconut starts to jab,
Remember the tales of this brave little lad.
With a shell for a helmet, a grin on his face,
Life's all about joy in this nutty place.

Tidal Whispers and Looming Dreams

The waves whispered secrets to the shore,
While crabs threw a party, oh what a score!
With a conch as a horn and shells as their seat,
They danced in the foam, such a wild beat.

A fish with a hat swam in with a wink,
Singing tunes that made everyone think.
'Join the fun, don't be such a bore!'
While dodging the seagulls who begged for more.

But a wise old turtle rolled over and said,
'Avoid those who munch on dreams while in bed.'
Yet crabs just shrugged, they were having a ball,
Claiming life is too good to just crawl.

As the sun sank low, one crab raised a toast,
To dreams that loom large, we love them the most!
With laughter and joy, they danced in the glow,
Building castles of sand as the tide said hello.

Aura of the Evening Mist

In the evening, the mist paints the sky,
While fireflies dance like stars way up high.
A monkey in pajamas swings from a tree,
Sipping on cocoa, so silly and free.

He spotted a gopher who wore shiny shoes,
Claiming they sparkled—no reason to snooze!
With laughter erupting, they played hopscotch,
Creating a game—if one fell, they'd botch.

A sloth named Larry just lounged on a branch,
While dreaming of parties and looking for a chance.
With a wink and a nod, he called out for fun,
For silly shenanigans have only begun.

So in the mist, where the whimsy is rife,
These creatures embrace all that's funny in life.
They twirl and they leap, in a merry old twist,
Making sweet memories in the evening mist.

Nestled in the Heart of Paradise

In a nook of the palm trees, laughter takes flight,
With monkeys in bow ties, all dressed up just right.
They cracked jokes with parrots, a colorful crew,
While sipping on smoothies both tangy and blue.

Alligators practiced their ballet routine,
Wearing tutus that sparkled, a real sight to glean.
With a croc as the maestro, they twirled with a flair,
As flamingos played pianos from their cozy lair.

A coconut crab held a stand-up show,
Joking 'bout crabs with no homes below.
With a punchline so bright, the crowd roared with glee,
Not even a snail could keep up with the spree!

As night crept in with a wink and a sigh,
Creatures of all kinds waved their goodbyes.
In the heart of this paradise, laughter's the key,
In a world full of wonders, there's still room to be free.

www.ingramcontent.com/pod-product-compliance
Lightning Source LLC
Chambersburg PA
CBHW072130070526
44585CB00016B/1606